Who Is the Best?

By Pauline Cartwright

Illustrated by Mary Lonsdale

ᕁ Dominie Press, Inc.

Publisher: Raymond Yuen
Project Editor: John S. F. Graham
Editor: Bob Rowland
Designer: Greg DiGenti
Illustrator: Mary Lonsdale

Published by:

₽ Dominie Press, Inc.

1949 Kellogg Avenue
Carlsbad, California 92008 USA

www.dominie.com

1-800-232-4570

Paperback ISBN 0-7685-1622-6
Printed in Singapore by PH Productions Pte Ltd
1 2 3 4 5 6 PH 05 04 03

Table of Contents

Chapter One
Competition Day

Lion could hear the animals arguing.

"I'm the biggest, so *I'm* the best," said one.

"No, *I'm* the best!" said another.

"I'm strongest, so *I'm* the best," said one.

"No, you're not!" said another.

All morning they argued about being fiercest, or fattest, or fastest, or furriest.

All afternoon they argued about being loudest, or longest, or loveliest.

All evening they argued about being greediest, or grandest, or greatest.

"So, *I'm* the best!"

"No, *I'm* the best!"

Then, at last, they went to sleep.

"Thank goodness for that," said Lion, and he went to sleep, too. But first, he said, "I think it is time for a Competition Day."

Chapter Two
I'm the Best!

Next morning, Lion called the animals together.

"I have listened to all of you arguing about who is the best at this, and the best at that, and the very best of all. I have decided it is time for a Competition

Day. That will settle the arguments, and you won't need to keep bickering."

Right away, some of the animals knew they didn't want to compete. They knew that Lion was very wise. They knew that they shouldn't be arguing.

They also knew it might be very hard to win Lion's competitions.

But some of the animals called out.

"I'm the best!"

"I'm the biggest!"

"I'm the brainiest!"

They pushed to the front of all the animals. They wanted to compete.

There was Monkey. He was always in the middle of everything.

There was Giraffe. She always knew what was going on because she could see over everyone's head.

There was Elephant. He picked up

Monkey in his trunk and put him in a tree. Elephant liked jokes.

There was Hippo. She was covered in mud.

There was Cheetah. He swished his tail and purred.

"Only five of you?" said Lion. "All

that fighting, and only five who want to compete? Imagine!"

Some of the animals hid their faces.

"The first competition," said Lion, "is a race to see who can run the fastest. Are you sure nobody else wants to enter?"

"No thank you," murmured most of the animals.

Chapter Three
Go! Go! Go!

"I'm good at running," said Monkey, and he jumped down from the tree.

"My legs are longest," smiled Giraffe.

"Running isn't my favorite thing," frowned Hippo.

"Look out for me!" trumpeted

Elephant. Everyone jumped.

Cheetah said nothing at all. He just kept purring.

Lion lined them up. "Ready, set, go!"

Off they went, and all the animals cried out, "Go! Go! Go!"

Cheetah won. He was way ahead of all the others.

Lion called out, "Cheetah is the fastest!" All the animals cheered.

Cheetah purred. "I told you I'm the best. Watch me win the next competition as well."

Lion said, "The second competition is a race to see who can climb the fastest."

He lined the animals up at the bottom of a high cliff.

"Watch me!" called Cheetah.

"Ready, set, go!" said Lion.

Hippo didn't even try. Giraffe started,

but the cliff was too steep. Elephant crashed through the trees and made a lot of noise and dust.

Cheetah ran between the trees. He leaped up the steep places. He was very fast.

But Monkey went faster! He leaped from one tree to the other. He got to the top first.

"Hooray!" cried all the animals.

"Monkey can climb the fastest!" Lion called out. All the animals cheered.

Chapter Four
Easy to Pick the Winner

Cheetah was mad because he thought he should have won. Hippo felt silly. She had been arguing that she was the best animal out of all the animals, but she hadn't won anything yet.

Lion said, "Are you five ready for the

next competition?"

"Yes," they answered.

Lion told all the other animals, "You are to call out when you can see which one can reach the highest."

"That's not fair," said Elephant. "Everyone knows that Giraffe is the tallest. She'll win."

Monkey said, "You haven't seen how high I can reach. I can climb up and up, and reach higher than Giraffe."

Lion said, "Ready, set, go!"

Elephant stuck his trunk up as high as he could. But he could see that Giraffe's neck was much taller than he could ever reach.

Cheetah just sat and watched. "I don't climb trees," he said.

Monkey jumped into the tree and hopped from branch to branch. But as he

got higher into the tree, he had to be more careful. The branches were very thin at the top of the tree and couldn't support his weight. He went as high as he could.

But Giraffe could reach higher just by extending her neck. She reached the leaves at the very top of the tree and looked down at Monkey.

"Giraffe! Giraffe! Giraffe!" called the animals.

Monkey wanted to win. "I can make it!" he shouted. He jumped the last few feet to the very top branches, but they were too small to hold him. A branch broke off in his hand, and he fell down, down until elephant caught him. Monkey felt a little sick from his fall.

Lion called out, "Giraffe is the winner!"

"I feel even sillier," said Hippo. She had tried, but she was not good at reaching up.

"Now we will see who can stay under the water the longest," said Lion.

All the animals gathered around a large pool.

Hippo liked this competition. She was so excited that she ran over ahead of the others and splashed into the water.

Elephant waded in after her. Cheetah went next, but he wasn't very happy. Swimming was all right, but staying under water wasn't Cheetah's idea of fun. Monkey was so unhappy, he ran up a tree and wouldn't get into the water at all.

"Everybody under... now!" called Lion.

Giraffe didn't go into water very often. She bent her long neck and put her head in for only a moment or two. Cheetah didn't stay under much longer. Elephant kept floating to the top! He laughed a lot.

But Hippo stayed under so long that all the animals thought she was never coming up. At last, she appeared.

"Hippo can stay under the water the longest of all!" called Lion

"Hooray!" called all the animals.

Hippo blushed.

Lion said, "Now we will see who can make the loudest noise."

He stood in front of the five animals who wanted to compete. "You can't make a noise all at once. You must take turns."

Cheetah went first. He looked as if he might make a loud noise, but his noise wasn't very loud at all. Monkey was smaller than Cheetah, but his noise was much bigger. Giraffe's noise was so soft that not many animals heard it.

"With that long neck," said Hippo, "I thought she would be able to do much better."

Hippo made an angry grunting noise that wasn't very loud, either.

Then Elephant put his trunk in the air and trumpeted. The noise was long and loud. Very loud! So loud that the other animals covered their ears.

"It's easy to pick the winner," said Lion. "Elephant is the one who can make the loudest noise."

Elephant trumpeted again, three times. Each time, the animals cheered.

Chapter Five
Step Forward

"**W**ell," said Lion, "the competitions
are over. Fastest runner, step forward."

Cheetah came forward.

"Fastest climber, step forward."

Monkey leaped out of a tree.

"The highest reach, step forward."

Giraffe needed to take only two steps with her long legs.

"You step forward, too, Hippo. You stayed the longest under water."

The last to join the line was Elephant.

"You can make the loudest noise, Elephant," said Lion.

Then Lion turned to the other animals. "So, which one of these is the best animal of all?" he asked.

No one could decide. They thought about it and talked about it.

Nobody knew.

"I'll tell you," said Lion.

"Please do," the animals said.

"All these animals are the best," he said.

"They can't *all* be the best," said Zebra.

"They are," said Lion. "You saw how each one is the best at something."

"We did," said the animals.

"That doesn't mean that they are better than each other. That doesn't mean that they are better than any of you. All of you are good at something. You, Zebra, are best at hiding in the tall grass. You, Snake, are the best at being quiet. You are all special in one way or

another."

"Lion is right," said Zebra.

Lion said, "Now go on home and don't argue any more. Always remember that everyone is special."

Quietly, the animals went home.

Chapter Six
Bat

Lion was about to follow them when Bat flew out of a hollow tree.

"I have been asleep," said Bat. "But I did hear some of that."

"Good," said Lion. "Then you'll know

why you shouldn't argue about who is best."

"Lion," said Bat, "I heard what you said about everyone being good at something. I don't think I am. I have thought and thought, but I'm not tall or strong. I'm so little. I can't jump or—"

"Bat," said Lion, "There is something you can do that none of the others can do."

"There is?"

"You can fly."

"But birds fly, too. How does that make me special?"

"You can fly in the darkness."

"But owls can fly in the darkness."

"But, Bat, you are a mammal. No other mammal can fly in the darkness. You are special."

Bat squeaked with delight. "I *am* special!"

"You are," said Lion. "So off you go, and always remember that everyone is special in one way or another."

"Thank you, Lion," said Bat. He flew off into the dusk. He squeaked as he went, "Everyone is special! Everyone is special!"

Suddenly he swooped around and flew back. He shouted out above Lion.

"And you are very special, Lion. You are the best at thinking."

"Thank you, Bat," said Lion.

Bat flew off again. Lion watched him until he was a tiny dot far away in the sky.

Then Lion went home across the plain, smiling as he went. It had been a very good Competition Day.